POWER OF
Passionistas

PLANNING YOUR PATH TO PURPOSE

POWER OF
Passionistas

PLANNING YOUR PATH TO PURPOSE

A GUIDED JOURNAL

Amy & Nancy Harrington
Passionistas Press

ISBN #979-8-9887226-1-8

This book is dedicated to
all our Passionista sisters,
who have been our inspiration
in uncovering our purpose
and making our mission a reality.

Velcome to *Planning Your Path to Purpose.*

n 2016, at the height of the #MeToo movement, we launched The Passionistas 'roject with a mission to support women. It started simply as a podcast giving omen a platform to share their unfiltered stories of following their passions, ıspiring others to do the same. Over time, our brand expanded to include a ubscription box featuring products from women-owned businesses and the nnual Power of Passionistas Women's Equity Summit. Despite our efforts to romote women, something felt amiss.

ı 2023, we received a pivotal piece of advice: we were driving down the road hile reading the map, destined to crash and burn if we continued. This velation prompted us to pause and reevaluate our mission. With the guidance f amazing coaches, we decided to take a hard look at the core of The assionistas Project. Our goal was clear — we wanted to help women — but were e truly addressing their needs or were we just doing what we do and hoping it ight serve our community?

'e needed to redefine our purpose. With the help of Brand Builder and eadership Coach Kylee Stone, we revisited the foundation of our project. She sked us, "What are your four key values? The words that define you and make ›u unique."

ıssion was undeniably at the heart of our vision. Inclusivity was another ›rnerstone of our work. As real-life sisters, we knew we wanted to share the nse of Sisterhood with all the women we connect with. But the fourth word uded us until we realized it was Purpose. For us, great passion comes with eat purpose, providing direction and meaning to our lives.

arifying our purpose has been transformative. It has helped us set goals and iorities, ultimately providing us with a sense of fulfillment and satisfaction. ıilding a business, focusing on self-improvement or having an impact on ciety is not always easy. Staying on track to realize your vision can be allenging. However, we have found that having clarity in our purpose has creased our motivation, resilience and overall well-being.

As we interviewed women and non-binary people for The Passionistas Project podcast and internet radio show, we noticed a recurring theme: fulfilling one's purpose. Many of the individuals we interviewed shared valuable tips they learned on their own personal explorations. We wanted to pass those along to you.

This guided journal is designed to help you discover your own life's purpose. We know this can be a deeply personal journey and sometimes feel burdensome. But from our own experience, we know that the load you bear can feel a little lighter when your sisters (born and chosen) are helping you carry the weight.

That's why we're sharing tips from women who have done their own exploration to find their purpose and learned important lessons along the way. This journal is not just a collection of quotes, prompts and exercises, it is a tool full of tips for you to take advantage of during your self-exploration, reflection and growth.

How to Use This Journal

On the pages that follow, you will read quotes from the passionate women in our sisterhood about how they found their purpose. Each pearl of wisdom is followed by a prompt to help you explore your own thoughts about purpose.

This is a 52-week journal that you can start on any date. There are 52 prompts — one for each week — and quarterly planners to keep you on track to meet your goals.

Reflecting on Your Journey So Far

To start, reflect on your journey up to this point. Consider the significant moments, achievements and challenges that have shaped who you are today. What experiences have brought you the most joy and fulfillment? Which challenges have taught you the most about yourself? Use these reflections as a foundation for exploring your purpose.

Exploring Your Values, Passions and Strengths

Next, take time to identify and reflect on your most important values. What do you stand for? What principles define your goals?

Our purpose sprang from our passion for helping other women. What are you most passionate about? What activities make you lose track of time? What topics could you talk about for hours? How does that passion fuel your sense of purpose?

Finally, what strengths and skills do you have that you can use as tools to help you fulfill your purpose? What are you naturally good at? What do others often come to you for help with?

Setting Purposeful Goals and Embracing the Journey

Once you have a clearer understanding of your values, passions and strengths, you can start setting goals that align with your purpose. These goals should be specific, actionable and aligned with your overall vision for your life.

Finding your purpose is not a one-time event but an ongoing journey. Embrace it with an open heart and mind. We hope this journal will be a valuable companion on your path to discovering and living your true purpose.

Stay passionate.
Amy & Nancy Harrington
Co-Founders of The Passionistas Project

CULTIVATING GRATITUDE IS A POWERFUL PRACTICE THAT CAN POSITIVELY IMPACT YOUR MINDSET AND OVERALL WELL-BEING. ENJOY THIS RITUAL AND WATCH HOW IT CONTRIBUTES TO FULFILLED LIFE.

(Day): (Month): (Year):

HEALTH

TRAVEL

CAREER

FINANCES

RELATIONSHIPS

SPIRITUALITY

NOTE: Download additional copies of this planner at www.thepassionistasproject.com/purpose-journal

RATE YOUR CURRENT SATISFACTION IN EACH AREA OF YOUR LIFE ON A SCALE OF 1–10, WITH 10 BEING THE HIGHEST. SHADE IN THE SATISFACTION POINTS IN EACH "SLICE" OF THE GRAPHIC.

(Day): *(Month):* *(Year):*

---

finance
family
romance
friends
career
study
hobby
recreation
health
fitness
emotional health
spirituality

Assess how satisfied you are with your life in each area.

OTE: Download additional copies of this planner at www.thepassionistasproject.com/purpose-journal

CULTIVATING GRATITUDE IS A POWERFUL PRACTICE THAT CAN POSITIVELY IMPACT YOUR MINDSET AND OVERALL WELL-BEING. ENJOY THIS RITUAL AND WATCH HOW IT CONTRIBUTES TO FULFILLED LIFE.

(Day):	*(Month):*	*(Year):*

Affirmation	*Inspiration*
Mood	*I'm grateful for*

(How I feel) *ESTABLISH A CONNECTION WITH YOUR THREE WORLDS (MENTAL / PHYSICAL / SPIRITUAL). SET AN INTENTION FOR EACH AND SHARE HOW YOU FEEL*

MENTAL

PHYSICAL

SPIRITUAL

NOTE: Download additional copies of this planner at www.thepassionistasproject.com/purpose-journal

GRATITUDE *planner*

:ULTIVATING GRATITUDE IS A POWERFUL PRACTICE THAT CAN POSITIVELY IMPACT YOUR MINDSET AND)VERALL WELL-BEING. ENJOY THIS RITUAL AND WATCH HOW IT CONTRIBUTES TO FULFILLED LIFE.

Day):	(Month):	(Year):

ffirmation	Inspiration
lood	I'm grateful for

lowI feel) ESTABLISH A CONNECTION WITH YOUR THREE WORLDS (MENTAL / PHYSICAL / SPIRITUAL). SET AN INTENTION FOR EACH AND SHARE HOW YOU FEEL

MENTAL

PHYSICAL

SPIRITUAL

TE: Download additional copies of this planner at www.thepassionistasproject.com/purpose-journal

"You are not stuck where you are, where you used to be or with what happened to you. You can make new choices."

DR. HOKEHE EKO
CEO, Glow Pediatrics and Kits of Hope, Inc.

Write about an area where you feel stuck and a choice you can make today to change the outcome.

“If you cannot go through the front door, go through the side window.”

LINDA HOLLANDER
CEO of Sponsor Concierge and Founder of the Sponsor Secrets Seminar

How can you look at a challenge you're struggling with from a different perspective?

"Don't 'should' all over yourself."

DARLENE HILDEBRANDT
Creator and Owner of Digital Photo Mentor

Make a list of the "shoulds" that you beat yourself up about and then give yourself the grace to let them go.

“Discovering your passion and purpose is a continuous journey where simply giving yourself permission to live passionately illuminates the path.”

KARSTA MARIE
Personal Development Coach,
Speaker and Award-Winning Author

Draw a treasure map showing all of the steps you've taken to realize your purpose and plot out your next three steps to reaching your goals.

"Get ahead of life before life gets ahead of you!"

CLAIRE JONES
Co-Founder of Sista Creatives Rising

Write about something that you need to get ahead of so life doesn't get ahead of you.

"Done is better than perfect."

MERCEDES BARBA
Publicist, Founder of Mercedes and Media

Write about a project that you could finish today but you've been putting off because it's not perfect.

"Confidence is not something for the elite. It is available to all of us."

JULIE DeLUCCA-COLLINS
Founder of Go Confidently Services,
Author, Speaker, Coach and Podcaster

Make a list of the things that are holding you back from feeling confident.

"I have to live this life so much to the fullest that when that last breath comes, I don't have any regrets."

CRYSTAL LYNESE WALKER
D&I Executive

Make a list of any regrets you have and commit to letting them go.

"Perseverance is more important than talent. It's more important than intelligence. That's who wins the game. You have to persevere."

BETH HARRINGTON
Filmmaker, Producer, Director and Writer

Cut out images or make a drawing of what perseverance means to you.

"There are times where we need to be heard and we need to roar."

JEN DALLAS
Founder, Jen Dallas Interiors Studio

Make a list of the unspoken topics that you are going to start roaring about.

"When I sit in my gratitude, I realize how much there really is already. That fuels my passion."

DIANA GRESHTCHUK
Founder and CEO of Fan Your Flame LLC

Make a list of all of the things you feel gratitude for and note how each fuels your passion.

“Your pain is not
your purpose.
It can shape you and
strengthen you,
but your purpose
was never meant
to be the pain you
experienced.”

TAMI IMLAY
International Women's Achievement Coach

Write about a pain point that has been impacting your journey and imagine what your life will look like when you release it.

"Discovering what lights you up is a journey. Being curious is the first step."

KATHY BARRON
Founder and Editor-in-Chief Women Who Podcast Magazine

Make a list of three things you're curious about. Spend 15 minutes doing research and write down an interesting fact about each one.

(Day):	*(Month):*	*(Year):*
What is your first memory?		
What are you most proud of?		
What is something I have overcome?		
What was the best present you've ever received?		
What's your favorite memory?		
Are you happy?		
What challenges are you currently facing?		
Do you feel content with life?		
What's your first thought when you wake up?		
What's your last thought before you go to sleep?		
Do you enjoy your life?		

NOTE: Download additional copies of this planner at www.thepassionistasproject.com/purpose-journal

(Day): *(Month):* *(Year):*

INTENTIONS	AFFIRMATION
NOURISHMENT	
SELF-CARE	WHAT MAKES RIGHT NOW GREAT
MOVEMENT	
GOALS	
OUTCOME I WANT TO ACHIEVE	NOTES
WHY IT IS IMPORTANT	
ACTION PLAN	

OTE: Download additional copies of this planner at www.thepassionistasproject.com/purpose-journal

CULTIVATING GRATITUDE IS A POWERFUL PRACTICE THAT CAN POSITIVELY IMPACT YOUR MINDSET AND OVERALL WELL-BEING. ENJOY THIS RITUAL AND WATCH HOW IT CONTRIBUTES TO FULFILLED LIFE.

(Day):	*(Month):*	*(Year):*

Affirmation	*Inspiration*
Mood	*I'm grateful for*

(How I feel) *ESTABLISH A CONNECTION WITH YOUR THREE WORLDS (MENTAL / PHYSICAL / SPIRITUAL). SET AN INTENTION FOR EACH AND SHARE HOW YOU FEEL*

MENTAL

PHYSICAL

SPIRITUAL

NOTE: Download additional copies of this planner at www.thepassionistasproject.com/purpose-journal

ULTIVATING GRATITUDE IS A POWERFUL PRACTICE THAT CAN POSITIVELY IMPACT YOUR MINDSET AND VERALL WELL-BEING. ENJOY THIS RITUAL AND WATCH HOW IT CONTRIBUTES TO FULFILLED LIFE.

Day): *(Month):* *(Year):*

ffirmation	*Inspiration*
Mood	*I'm grateful for*

How I feel) *ESTABLISH A CONNECTION WITH YOUR THREE WORLDS (MENTAL / PHYSICAL / SPIRITUAL). SET AN INTENTION FOR EACH AND SHARE HOW YOU FEEL*

MENTAL

PHYSICAL

SPIRITUAL

TE: Download additional copies of this planner at www.thepassionistasproject.com/purpose-journal

"To discover what you're passionate about, spend time thinking about what brings you joy and satisfaction. Then share it and find your community."

NATALIE KIME
Financial Professional

Make a list of the things that bring you joy and places where you can go to connect with people who share that interest.

"See what's there instead of what's missing."

MELODY GODFRED
The Self Love Philosopher

When you look at your life, what fulfills you the most?

"When you're led by passion, that translates into power."

DANAY ESCANAVERINO
CEO of LunaSol Media and Founder of Mira.Click

Make a list of all of the superpowers you derive from following your passion.

"Fueled by an intense passion, I am committed to dismantling ableist structures, refusing to tolerate hypocrisy, gaslighting or disrespect toward people with disabilities."

SELENE LUNA
Actor and Film Producer

Make a list of the issues you are committed to and what fuels your passion for each of them.

"Sometimes your purpose is dropped on you like a ton of bricks but it's a journey to find your passion. Keep going."

CAROLYN KOPPEL
Aaron's Mom and Founder of Aaron's Coffee Corner

Write about an unexpected moment or experience in your life that has led you to defining your purpose.

"When you find your purpose in life, it is the most peaceful place to live."

LORI LYNN
Creator of Overall Buddies, Singer/Songwriter and Speaker

Write about your purpose in life and how it makes you feel.

"It will all work out — one way or the other. It might not be the outcome you expect, but it always works out the way it should."

NANCY HARRINGTON
Co-Founder of The Passionistas Project

Write down three things you were worried about when you were 15.

NOTE: If you can't remember them, that's the point. When we were little, our mother always used to say, "You're never going to remember this when you're older..." She was usually right.)

"You can be the juiciest, ripest peach and there will still be people who don't like peaches."

SANTINA MUHA
Actor, Writer and Storyteller

Write about the way you react when people just don't get you and how you can adjust your response to handle the rejection.

"Be a starfish. Always find a way to regrow."

CinDiLo
Midlife Author

Write about an area where you feel stunted and ways in which you can grow in a new direction to address it.

"Women who know their worth and use their voice are on fire."

JEN RAFFERTY
Founder of Empowered Educator

Make a list of the women you know that are "on fire." How do you draw inspiration from them?

"I really try to see the good in people and I really try to have fun."

KATIE CHIN
Founder of Wok Star Catering and
Award-Winning Cookbook Author

Make a collage of activities that you like to do to have fun and recharge your batteries.

"I was capable of more, so I just kept putting one hand above the other."

LISA THOMPSON
Mountaineering Coach, Author and Speaker

Make a list of times you thought you weren't capable of something that you were able to achieve.

"Decide what it is that you need most in this world and go do that."

SUZ CARPENTER
Founder of CarpenterOne80

What is the one thing that you want to go after and what are some things you can do to get it?

(Day): (Month): (Year):

I LOVE THAT I AM:
I AM PROUD OF:
I AM INSPIRED BY:
I FEEL CONFIDENT WHEN I:

NOTE: Download additional copies of this planner at www.thepassionistasproject.com/purpose-journal

(Day): (Month): (Year):

I AM:	I AM NOT:
I WILL:	I WILL NOT:
I CAN:	I CANNOT:
I WANT:	I DO NOT WANT:

OTE: Download additional copies of this planner at www.thepassionistasproject.com/purpose-journal

CULTIVATING GRATITUDE IS A POWERFUL PRACTICE THAT CAN POSITIVELY IMPACT YOUR MINDSET AND OVERALL WELL-BEING. ENJOY THIS RITUAL AND WATCH HOW IT CONTRIBUTES TO FULFILLED LIFE.

(Day):	*(Month):*	*(Year):*

Affirmation	*Inspiration*
Mood	*I'm grateful for*

(How I feel) *ESTABLISH A CONNECTION WITH YOUR THREE WORLDS (MENTAL / PHYSICAL / SPIRITUAL). SET AN INTENTION FOR EACH AND SHARE HOW YOU FEEL*

MENTAL

PHYSICAL

SPIRITUAL

NOTE: Download additional copies of this planner at www.thepassionistasproject.com/purpose-journal

GRATITUDE *planner*

ULTIVATING GRATITUDE IS A POWERFUL PRACTICE THAT CAN POSITIVELY IMPACT YOUR MINDSET AND VERALL WELL-BEING. ENJOY THIS RITUAL AND WATCH HOW IT CONTRIBUTES TO FULFILLED LIFE.

Day): *(Month):* *(Year):*

ffirmation	*Inspiration*
lood	*I'm grateful for*

low I feel) *ESTABLISH A CONNECTION WITH YOUR THREE WORLDS (MENTAL / PHYSICAL / SPIRITUAL). SET AN INTENTION FOR EACH AND SHARE HOW YOU FEEL*

MENTAL

PHYSICAL

SPIRITUAL

E: Download additional copies of this planner at www.thepassionistasproject.com/purpose-journal

"Show up, care about what you're doing and be curious."

NAN KOHLER
Owner of Grist & Toll

Make a list of topics that peak your curiosity that you want to learn more about.

"Do something nice, be kind and learn."

ERICA WRIGHT
Founder of Project U First

Block out one hour a week to focus on learning something new to advance your goal. Make a list of actions you can take during those times.

"Chop wood, carry water. What is the next thing in front of me to do?"

JESSICA CRAVEN
Activist, Author and TikTok Creator

What's the next task in front of you to help you achieve your goal?

"I recommit myself every day to being unstoppable."

JOAN BAKER
Co-Founder and VP SOVAS™,
Executive Producer and Host: That's Voiceover!
and The Voice Arts® Awards

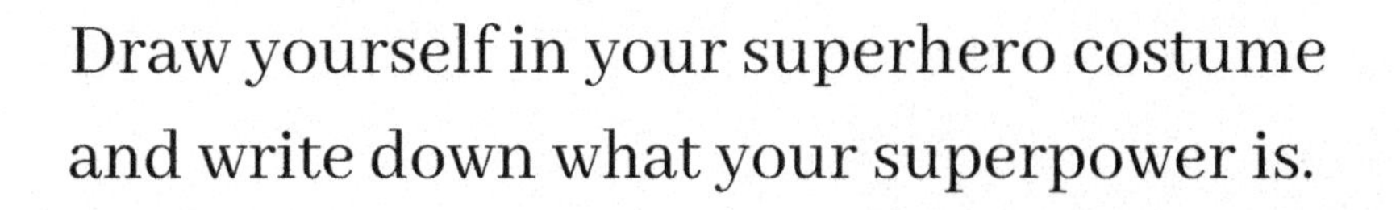

Draw yourself in your superhero costume and write down what your superpower is.

"You only have one body. You have to be mindful in how you care for it — physically, mentally, emotionally and spiritually."

KAREN ARCENEAUX
Get Karenated® Dance and Fitness LLC, Founder and CEO

What have you been ignoring about your self-care? Make a list and then take the time to schedule the appointments you need.

"It's not a question of if, it's a question of when."

LINDSAY GORDON
Career Coach

Write about something you're working on that you believe will happen and the steps you can take to continue to move it forward.

“It’s going to get done with calm.”

MICHELLE DANNER
Filmmaker and Acting Coach

Write about a time when you were able to achieve more from a place of calm rather than chaos.

"The only thing that matters is persistence."

SASHEE CHANDRAN
Founder and CEO of Tea Drops

Write about something you are considering giving up. What would happen if you stayed persistent and saw it through?

“Don’t let other people tell you ‘no.’”

CARA REEDY
Director, Disabled Journalists Association

What are you hearing "no" about? Write about ways in which you can move forward until you get a "yes."

"There's no right way of doing it, there's just your way of doing it. So don't let that stop you."

DIA BONDI
Founder and CEO of Dia Bondi Communications

What's one thing you do that makes you unique from everyone else you know?

"In order to live a good life, you must do good."

MAE CHANDRAN
Cook, Gardner and Mother

Bake cookies, write a note or bring flowers from your garden to a neighbor. Describe their reaction below.

"The more we thrive, the more we can give others the support and opportunity to thrive themselves."

AMY HARRINGTON
Co-Founder of The Passionistas Project

Make a list of the people that you commit to helping to thrive.

"If your dream only includes you, it's too small."

DeMANE DAVIS
Film and Television Director and Producer

Make a list of all of the people who you'd like to include in building your dream and theirs.

(Day): *(Month):* *(Year):*

(Overview)

SUMMARIZE YOUR KEY EVENTS AND ACCOMPLISHMENTS.

(Achievements)

WHAT WERE YOUR MAJOR ACHIEVEMENTS ?

(Gratitude) LIST THREE THINGS YOU'RE GRATEFUL FOR

IDENTIFY KEY PRIORITIES AND YOUR NEXT SET OF GOALS

- ○ ______
- ○ ______
- ○ ______
- ○ ______
- ○ ______

◉ TO START ○ OK ○ DELAY ○ STUCK ○ CANCEL

NOTE: Download additional copies of this planner at www.thepassionistasproject.com/purpose-journal

REVIEW MY *reflections*

(Day): (Month): (Year):

MY TOP 5 ACCOMPLISHMENTS

- ○
- ○
- ○
- ○
- ○

THINGS I HAVE TO LEARN

- ○
- ○
- ○
- ○
- ○

THINGS I HAVE TO CHANGE

- ○
- ○
- ○
- ○
- ○

NEXT PRIORITIES

- ○
- ○
- ○
- ○
- ○

NOTE: Download additional copies of this planner at www.thepassionistasproject.com/purpose-journal

CULTIVATING GRATITUDE IS A POWERFUL PRACTICE THAT CAN POSITIVELY IMPACT YOUR MINDSET AND OVERALL WELL-BEING. ENJOY THIS RITUAL AND WATCH HOW IT CONTRIBUTES TO FULFILLED LIFE.

(Day): (Month): (Year):

Affirmation	Inspiration
Mood	I'm grateful for

(How I feel) ESTABLISH A CONNECTION WITH YOUR THREE WORLDS (MENTAL / PHYSICAL / SPIRITUAL). SET AN INTENTION FOR EACH AND SHARE HOW YOU FEEL

MENTAL

PHYSICAL

SPIRITUAL

NOTE: Download additional copies of this planner at www.thepassionistasproject.com/purpose-journal

GRATITUDE *planner*

ULTIVATING GRATITUDE IS A POWERFUL PRACTICE THAT CAN POSITIVELY IMPACT YOUR MINDSET AND VERALL WELL-BEING. ENJOY THIS RITUAL AND WATCH HOW IT CONTRIBUTES TO FULFILLED LIFE.

Day):	(Month):	(Year):

ffirmation	Inspiration
Mood	I'm grateful for

low I feel) ESTABLISH A CONNECTION WITH YOUR THREE WORLDS (MENTAL / PHYSICAL / SPIRITUAL). SET AN INTENTION FOR EACH AND SHARE HOW YOU FEEL

MENTAL

PHYSICAL

SPIRITUAL

TE: Download additional copies of this planner at www.thepassionistasproject.com/purpose-journal

"Be a light that encourages others to see the light that shines so brightly within them."

CAIRO EUBANKS
Founder, CairoSpeaks/CairoWrites

Write about what ignites the light in you and how you can use that to inspire others.

“The words that we say are a lifeline or an invitation for other people to say the things they might not be able to say.”

MAYA ENISTA SMITH
President, Thoughtful Human

Write about an aspect of yourself that you don't talk about but might help others open up if you share more.

"When we come together and hold each other and connect wherever we're at, then we can start to figure out ways to move through whatever mess is burning around us."

DR. MELISSA BIRD
CEO of Dr. Melissa Bird

Make a list of the women who share your vision. How you can be of support to them and how can they support you?

"Somebody put me on their shoulders and helped me rise and it's my responsibility to reach back and pull up. That's what we women do for each other."

SONALI PERERA BRIDGES
Founder and President, Shero's Rise

Reach out to three women and girls in your life and ask them how you can pull them up and help them achieve their goals.

“Realize there’s a whole network of a universe around you.”

HOLLY BERRY
Creative Director of A Natural Design

Draw a picture of all the wonders in the universe around you that inspire you to achieve your goals.

"The quality of your life is determined by your relationships."

VEE CHRISTIAN
Owner of Vee Mindful

Write about the relationships that are most important to you and how they enrich your life.

"Everything you need to be the best possible leader is within you."

KYLEE STONE
Brand Builder and Leadership Coach

Make a list of the qualities that make you a great leader.

"Discover the power within — because there's so much potential. Can you imagine if we all owned what we have within us?"

DALI RIVERA
Bullying Awareness and Prevention Educator

Make a list of the qualities that are within you to help you reach your potential.

"Truly live your life for you and live it with love instead of external worth."

LAUREN BEST
Mindset and Business Consultant, Certified Hypnotherapist and Provoker of Possibility

What can you do to ensure that you are truly living your life for you?

"Be happy and satisfied and fulfilled in your day-to-day, while building towards the future that you want."

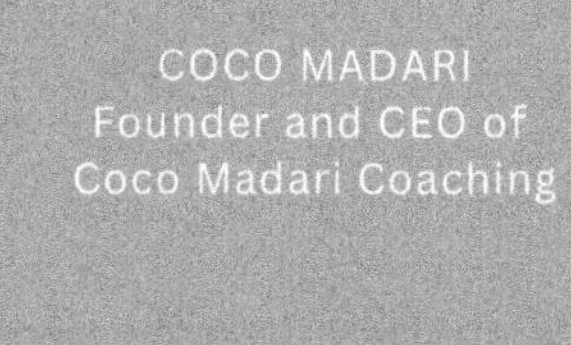

COCO MADARI
Founder and CEO of
Coco Madari Coaching

Make a list of what makes you happy and satisfied in your day-to-day life now.

"See the beauty you have within yourself."

CRISTINA GONZALEZ
The Curvy Girl Dating Coach

Make a list of the qualities that you feel are beautiful within you.

"We get to love life on our terms."

ANNMARIE ENTNER
Rheumatoid Arthritis Mindset Coach

Make a list of the things that you love about your life.

“We are what we’ve been waiting for.”

KIM ROXIE
CEO and Founder, LAMIK Beauty

What are you waiting for? Make a list of five things you can do to realize your purpose now.

CULTIVATING GRATITUDE IS A POWERFUL PRACTICE THAT CAN POSITIVELY IMPACT YOUR MINDSET AND OVERALL WELL-BEING. ENJOY THIS RITUAL AND WATCH HOW IT CONTRIBUTES TO FULFILLED LIFE.

(Day): (Month): (Year):

Affirmation	Inspiration
Mood	I'm grateful for

(How I feel) ESTABLISH A CONNECTION WITH YOUR THREE WORLDS (MENTAL / PHYSICAL / SPIRITUAL). SET AN INTENTION FOR EACH AND SHARE HOW YOU FEEL

MENTAL

PHYSICAL

SPIRITUAL

NOTE: Download additional copies of this planner at www.thepassionistasproject.com/purpose-journal

CULTIVATING GRATITUDE IS A POWERFUL PRACTICE THAT CAN POSITIVELY IMPACT YOUR MINDSET AND OVERALL WELL-BEING. ENJOY THIS RITUAL AND WATCH HOW IT CONTRIBUTES TO FULFILLED LIFE.

(Day):	*(Month):*	*(Year):*

Affirmation	*Inspiration*
Mood	*I'm grateful for*

(How I feel) *ESTABLISH A CONNECTION WITH YOUR THREE WORLDS (MENTAL / PHYSICAL / SPIRITUAL). SET AN INTENTION FOR EACH AND SHARE HOW YOU FEEL*

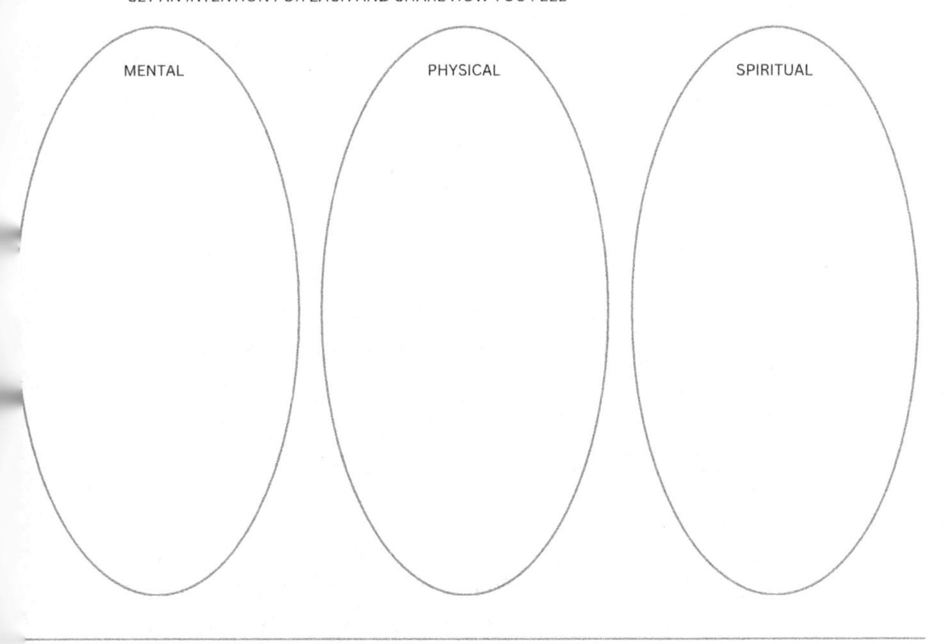

OTE: Download additional copies of this planner at www.thepassionistasproject.com/purpose-journal

RATE YOUR CURRENT SATISFACTION IN EACH AREA OF YOUR LIFE ON A SCALE OF 1–10, WITH 10 BEING THE HIGHEST. SHADE IN THE SATISFACTION POINTS IN EACH "SLICE" OF THE GRAPHIC

(Day): *(Month):* *(Year):*

finance
family
romance
friends
career
study
hobby
recreation
health
fitness
emotional health
spirituality

How has your wheel of life changed from the first time you did this exercise at the beginning of the journal?

NOTE: Download additional copies of this planner at www.thepassionistasproject.com/purpose-journal

Day): (Month): (Year):

☐	______	☐	______
☐	______	☐	______
☐	______	☐	______
☐	______	☐	______
☐	______	☐	______
☐	______	☐	______
☐	______	☐	______
☐	______	☐	______
☐	______	☐	______
☐	______	☐	______
☐	______	☐	______
☐	______	☐	______
☐	______	☐	______
☐	______	☐	______
☐	______	☐	______
☐	______	☐	______
☐	______	☐	______
☐	______	☐	______

TE: Download additional copies of this planner at www.thepassionistasproject.com/purpose-journal

CONTRIBUTING *passionistas*

KAREN ARCENEAUX, Get Karenated® Dance and Fitness LLC, Founder and CEO

With outrageous energy and passion, Karen's mission is to inspire self-confidence, uplift the human spirit and promote a healthy lifestyle through dance, fitness and nutrition. She teaches and trains to inspire... to transform. As a master instructor of the Lester Horton dance technique, NASM certified personal trainer and AFAA certified group fitness trainer, professional dancer and choreographer, she joyously fulfills her mission daily. *www.getkarenated.com*

JOAN BAKER, Co-Founder/VP SOVAS™, Executive Producer & Host: That's Voiceover! & The Voice Arts® Awards

Joan is an author, actor, voiceover artist, on-camera host and juror fo the Emmy® Awards at the Television Academy. She is the Co-founder and Vice President of the Society of Voice Arts and Sciences™ (SOVAS™), an international nonprofit corporation that oversees That's Voiceover!™ Career Expo, the Voice Arts® Awards and multiple programs providing training, education, academic/financial aid scholarships and career counseling for voice actors. *www.sovas.org*

MERCEDES BARBA, Publicist, Founder of Mercedes & Media

Mercedes is the Founder and Owner of Mercedes and Media, a publicity firm dedicated to helping entrepreneurs harness the powe of media to establish credibility, increase their visibility and attract clients to their businesses. With 15 years of experience and an Emmy nomination to her name, Mercedes' vision is to underscore that the media is an invaluable asset accessible to every entrepreneur. Its unparalleled potential for business owners, combined with Mercede industry insights and strategies, empowers entrepreneurs to unlock their own opportunities for securing media features. *www.mercedesbarba.com*

KATHY BARRON, Founder and Editor-in-Chief Women Who Podcast Magazine

Kathy is the Founder and Editor-in-Chief of Women Who Podcast magazine. Her mission is to increase the number of women podcaste by providing a mentorship program, learning community and a safe and supportive space for podcasters. *womenwhopodcastmag.com*

HOLLY BERRY, Creative Director of A Natural Design

Holly grew up on the Pacific Coast. Her love of learning is matched by her love for being outdoors. Her work in design started while she attended Seattle School of Visual Concepts. Her Bachelor of Science is in business management. She is Creative Director and Floral Designer at A Natural Design. *www.aNaturalDesign.com*

LAUREN BEST, Mindset and Business Consultant, Certified Hypnotherapist, Provoker of Possibility

Lauren is a Transformation Designer and Strategist, Certified Hypnotherapist, Multi-Best Selling Author and Host of the podcast Provoking Possibilities. She is also the Founder of Possibilities Universe, which is a place for people to discover tools and experiences to unlock possibility within a universe of self-discovery, celebration, creativity, curiosity and imperfection. *www.lauren-best.com*

DR. MELISSA BIRD, CEO of Dr. Melissa Bird

Melissa is a descendant of the Shivwits Band of Paiutes. She is a nationally recognized lay preacher, author and podcaster. She inspires personal understanding through contemplation, helps people use their intuition to change their lives and communities and encourages the healing of grief and loss through spiritual connection. She lives and works in Corvallis, Oregon, where she can often be found drinking Earl Gray tea with heavy cream while reading and waxing poetic about the beauty of life and love. *www.drmelissabird.com*

DIA BONDI, Founder and CEO of Dia Bondi Communications

Dia is the Founder and CEO of Dia Bondi Communications, a leadership communications firm helping founders and transformational leaders find their voice and lead with it. Dia's work aligns and activates people, teams and culture toward shared goals, making it possible for leaders to elevate impact and use communications as a strike point for their leadership. *www.diabondi.com*

SONALI PERERA BRIDGES, Founder and President, Shero's Rise

Sonali is an award-winning, dynamic, innovative leader with over 20 years of experience in a wide breadth of educational settings and the driving force behind Shero's Rise. She is the Founder and President of Bridges Educational Consulting, which provides college counseling for students, curriculum development and training for school districts and strategic enrollment management planning to institutions of higher education. *www.sherosrise.org*

SUZ CARPENTER, Founder of CarpenterOne80
Suz is a teacher, mentor and consultant. She created CarpenterOne80 to equip people with the tools they need to help them lose weight while living a lifestyle they love. Most people want to lose weight, usually to feel more confident in some area of their life. Her CarpenterOne80 blueprint is to turn people's lives 180 degrees toward the lifestyle they desire. *www.carpenterone80.com*

MAE CHANDRAN, Wife, Mother, Cook, Gardener
Mae was born in Canton, China and immigrated to Fall River, Massachusetts, where her family had a Chinese-American Restaurant. Mae overcame a dysfunctional family life when she fled to the West Coast to attend UCLA where she met her husband from Sri Lanka. Married for 48 years, they have two grown children and two grandchildren. Her accolades in cooking include twice winning the International Silver Award in a UK marmalade competition where over 3,000 jars of marmalade are received from all over the world. She was one of the contestants in the third season of *The Great American Recipe*.

SASHEE CHANDRAN, Founder and CEO of Tea Drops
Sashee is founder of Tea Drops, which creates bagless whole leaf teas, which sheds less waste than traditional tea bag packaging. Tea Drops has become a favorite among new and experienced tea drinkers alike, launching innovative tea experiences that merge flavorful blends, food art and innovation. Sashee is a 2021 Inc 100 Female Founder and a first place $100K Tory Burch Fellow Grant winner. *www.myteadrop.com*

KATIE CHIN, Author, Television Chef and Caterer
Katie, award-winning cookbook author, television chef, food blogger, caterer and Culinary Ambassador to the National Pediatric Cancer Foundation, has a passion for Asian food and is committed to teaching the American public that the very best Asian cooking can be achieved in a real home kitchen by real people on real schedules. *www.chefkatiechin.com*

VEE CHRISTIAN, Owner of Vee Mindful
Vee Mindful is a Certified Relationship Coach and published author who helps her clients attract love and keep it. Her tagline is Catch Flights and Feelings because she believes that if you truly want to get to know a person, then take a trip with them. *www.VeeMindful.com*

CinDiLo, Midlife Author
CinDiLo is passionate about helping women navigate their midlife awakening and rescue themselves: mind, body and soul. As a midlife author, blogger and well-being advocate, she believes it's important to nurture your dreams, your health and your heart. CinDiLo believes our generation is changing "the changes" and we do that by lifting ourselves up, while also lifting one another. *msha.ke/cindilo*

JESSICA CRAVEN, Activist, Author and TikTok Creator
Jessica is a community organizer, activist, mom and elected member of the Los Angeles County Democratic Party. She's also the author of "Chop Wood, Carry Water," a daily actions e-mail that's been published five days a week since November of 2016. She's a member of the CADem Environmental Caucus, a climate activist and a grassroots volunteer who has knocked doors, phone-banked, fundraised, texted and postcarded for hundreds of progressive candidates. *tinyurl.com/cwcwsubscribe*

JEN DALLAS, Founder, Jen Dallas Interiors Studio
Characterized by her personalized approach and creativity, Jen Dallas melds sophistication and history in creating the design of each project. Jen goes far beyond the traditional designer; carefully collaborating and incorporating her client's nature as a whole; their purpose, aspirations and goals to make a positive change in the home, office and garden. Her namesake studio based in Santa Monica, California has their own line of products including textiles, matching ceramic tiles, lighting and an upcoming rug collection. *www.jendallas.com www.maplejude.com*

MICHELLE DANNER, Filmmaker and Acting Coach
Michelle is a legendary acting teacher. Her students have included Christian Slater, Salma Hayek, Gerard Butler, Seth MacFarlane and Penelope Cruz. She is the director of the feature film *Miranda's Victim*, which stars Ryan Phillippe, Luke Wilson, Donald Sutherland, Mireille Enos andy Garcia, Abigail Breslin, Emily VanCamp, Josh Bowman and others. Michelle runs The Creative Center for the Arts in Culver City. *www.michelledanner.com*

DeMANE DAVIS, Film and TV Director and Producer
DeMane is a Film and TV Director and Producer who has helmed many episodes of TV including *Queen Sugar*, *How To Get Away with Murder*, *Station 19*, *YOU*, *Clarice* (the TV sequel to *The Silence of the Lambs*), the NAACP Image Award Winning Limited Series, *Self Made: Inspired by The Life of Madam CJ Walker* and the series, *Found* and *Brilliant Minds*. *www.demanedavis.com*

JULIE DeLUCCA-COLLINS, Founder of Go Confidently Services, Author, Speaker, Coach and Podcaster
As a Business and Life Strategist Coach, Julie helps women business owners launch or grow their businesses, get clients, be productive and achieve their dreams. Julie helps her clients create simple habits to achieve goals and change their lives. She is certified as a coach in Cognitive Behavioral Techniques, Holistic Coach, Tiny Habits, Social Emotional Learning Facilitator and a Thrive Global Coach.
www.goconfidentlycoaching.com

DR. HOKEHE EKO, CEO, Glow Pediatrics and Kits of Hope, Inc.
Dr. Eko, Mom, Board Certified Pediatrician, TedX Speaker, Author and CEO of Glow Pediatrics PLLC, partners with parents of children with ADHD/Autism to address the root causes of their children's behaviors so they GLOW with health from the inside out.She is also CEO of Kits of Hope, a 501 (3) organization, sharing love, hope and dignity with children in foster care. *www.glowpediatrics.com*

MAYA ENISTA SMITH, President, Thoughtful Human
Maya is President of Thoughtful Human, the plastic-free, plantable card company, which helps people find honest ways to communicate in dynamic relationships and challenging life circumstances. Prior to that she served as founding Executive Director of Lady Gaga's Born This Way Foundation for over a decade, where she worked to empower young people to create a kinder, braver world and be a source for mental health support. www.*thoughtfulhuman.co*

ANNMARIE ENTNER, Rheumatoid Arthritis Mindset Coach
Annmarie is an RA warrior turned RA and Autoimmune Support Coach, who knows all too well how an autoimmune diagnosis can be life-altering and turn your world upside down. After her own diagnosis and healing journey from RA began, she noticed the massive missing link in the healing process for patients with an autoimmune condition. Annmarie is the RA/autoimmune confidant for people as they navigate the beginning of their healing journey.
www.lifecoachingforchange.com/services

DANAY ESCANAVERINO, CEO of LunaSol Media and Founder of Mira.Click
Danay is an award-winning Latina serial entrepreneur, speaker and community builder. As CEO of boutique digital agency LunaSol Media, she connects brands to Latino consumers delivering millions of leads and sales to her clients. A Cuban immigrant and the daughter of a political prisoner, Danay is fiercely passionate about elevating the Latino community. As founder of LatinaMeetup she has introduced thousands of Latina brands to millions of consumers.
www.lunasolmedia.com

CAIRO EUBANKS, CEO of CairoSpeaks/CairoWrites
Cairo specializes in project implementation consulting, leadership development coaching and instructor-led trainings. An ICF-accredited Executive and Leadership Development Coach, Cairo has used her expertise as a coach and global citizen to design the curriculum for Bringing the Globe, an education technology company that provides resources in the areas of leadership development, advocacy and cultural exchange. *www.cairospeaks.com*

MELODY GODFRED, The Self Love Philosopher
Melody is an author, poet and speaker devoted to inspiring people to love themselves and transform their lives. She is the bestselling author of *Self Love Poetry: for Thinkers & Feelers, The ABCs of Self Love and* award-nominated *The Shift: Poetry for a New Perspective. www.melodygodfred*

CRISTINA GONZALEZ, The Curvy Girl Dating Coach
Cristina is a dating coach for curvy women who are ready to experience self love, embrace their single life and feel confident dating. She became a certified Life Coach and is on a mission to help every single woman live life every day feeling sexy, bold and owning it. *www.thecurvygirldatingcoach.com*

LINDSAY GORDON, Career Coach
Lindsay is a Forbes award-winning career coach, author and speaker on a mission to help people stop doing what they think is "right" in their career and start doing what's right for them. Through her work, she assists leaders in making clear and confident decisions so they can move forward with purpose. Lindsay loves baking complicated pastries, barbershop singing and applying her engineering brain to helping people be DECIDED. *www.alifeofoptions.com*

DIANA GRESHTCHUK, Founder and CEO, Fan Your Flame LLC
Diana (She/Her) is the Founder and CEO of Fan Your Flame LLC, a financial literacy coach and your best financial friend. She is passionately committed to guiding entrepreneurs, businesses and individuals to achieve a wide variety of financial goals. Diana utilizes pioneering methods rooted in practical financial/business concepts, emotional intelligence and mindset work to educate and empower her clients to achieve goals of financial independence, transformation and abundance. *www.fan-your-flame.com*
Photo: Bernadette Marciniak

BETH HARRINGTON, Filmmaker, Producer, Director and Writer

Beth is an independent producer, director and writer, whose fervor for American history, music and culture has led to a series of award-winning and critically acclaimed films. Whether exploring the aftermath of the eruption of Mount Pinatubo, chronicling the history of the Aleutian Islands or drinking up the world of craft beer brewing Beth seamlessly straddles the line between objective journalistic integrity and a passion for every subject. As a result, her films are both thought provoking and heartfelt. *www.bethharrington.com*

DARLENE HILDEBRANDT, Creator and Owner of Digital Photo Mentor

Darlene is a professional photographer who has photographed everything from food, editorial, products, portraits, weddings and events. Currently she prefers doing street and travel photography, bu still considers herself a people photographer first and foremost. She's been sharing her skills and experiences through articles on her website, video tutorials on her YouTube channel and photography classes and workshops. *www.digitalphotomentor.com*

LINDA HOLLANDER, CEO of Sponsor Concierge and Founder of the Sponsor Secrets Seminar

Linda Hollander has over 20 years of experience as a small business owner and as the industry leader in teaching people how to tap into the awesome power of corporate sponsors. She's the author of the number one bestseller "Corporate Sponsorship in Three Easy Steps." She's also th CEO of Sponsor Concierge and the Founder of the Sponsor Secrets Seminar. *www.sponsorconcierge.com*

TAMI IMLAY, International Women's Achievement Coach

Tami is an Air Force Veteran turned Executive Coach, International Speaker and Author who has used her journey of overcoming adversity to inspire others to do the same. She loves traveling and hanging out with her family when she is not recording an episode fo her podcast *The Full Weight of Joy.*
www.tamimariecoaching.com/media/

CLAIRE JONES, Co-Founder of Sista Creatives Rising

A Buddhist and Frances Perkins Scholar, Claire's journey to scholarship began during her childhood in Barbados when she soug relief from living under domestic violence. Claire uses her creative works, writings and her mother-daughter project Sista Creatives Rising to encourage women trauma-survivors to utilize art for self-improvement. *www.sistacreativesrising.com*

Photo: Amaranthia Sepia

NATALIE KIME, Financial Professional
Natalie is a Financial Professional and is passionate about helping others achieve their financial goals, create the life of their dreams and leave a legacy behind.She takes pride in removing the emotion that can often be tied to financial conversations, bringing empathy and heart to her work. Her goal to ensure clients never have to make a choice of less than due to their financial situation and they and their loved ones can retire well and live with dignity. @NatalieMcPhieKime

NAN KOHLER, Owner of Grist & Toll
Nan is the owner of Grist & Toll, an urban flour mill in Pasadena, California. After spending years in the wine industry, Nan turned back to her first love, baking and was inspired to become a pioneer of the local whole grain movement. Grist & Toll is a resource for top quality freshly milled flour, an exploration of wheat, milling and baking and an unapologetic rejection of the status quo. *www.gristandtoll.com*

CAROLYN KOPPEL, Aaron's Mom and Founder of Aaron's Coffee Corner
Carolyn is currently Aaron's primary caregiver and runs all aspects of the non-profit organization Aaron's Coffee Corner. She has a background in journalism and television production coordination. She has worked for Viacom Television, Steven Spielberg's The Shoah Foundation and *The Oprah Winfrey Show*, among others.
www.aaronscoffeecorner.org
Photo: Ari Kobb

SELENE LUNA, Actor and Film Producer
Selene Luna played Soledad on FX's *Mayans M.C.* and the voice of Tía Rosita in Disney-Pixar's Academy Award and Golden Globe Award winner *Coco and* can be seen on Hulu's *Dragstravaganza*. Currently, Luna is the voice of Robin on Apple TV's animated series, *Frog and Toad*. Combining her talents in stage, screen and production, Selene Luna is the face of a new revolution in Hollywood.
www.seleneluna.com

LORI LYNN, Children's Singer/Songwriter
Lori Lynn is not only a singer/songwriter, but she is also an international speaker with a master's degree in education. She has over 15 years of successful experience conducting quality and engaging early childhood professional development. Lori Lynn is a certified Early Childhood PBIS Trainer and has worked as an adjunct early childhood instructor at the University of Nebraska, Omaha and Iowa Western Community College. *www.overallbuddies.com*

COCO MADARI, Founder and CEO of Coco Madari Coaching
Coco Madari is a BIPOC, queer, multi-talented, creative being who helps HSP (Highly Sensitive Person) creatives manage their projects and endeavors without overwhelm. They are also a music producer, singer/songwriter, visual artist, poet and DJ, living on the unsurrendered land of the Tsunemu First Nation (Colonial name: Nanaimo). *www.linkedin.com/in/cocomadari*

KARSTA MARIE, Personal Development Coach, Speaker and Award-Winning Author
Karsta Marie is a professional speaker, award-winning author, podcast host and coach with over two decades of experience. After enduring a life that was "fine" for years, she embarked on a mid-life awakening journey. Now, she empowers women to overcome limiting beliefs and live life by design, not default. *www.karstamarie.com*
Photo: Autumn Lee

SANTINA MUHA, Actor, Writer, Storyteller
Santina is a Sicilian Jersey Cali girl who can be seen in several films and TV shows, as well as on comedy stages on both coasts. Her roles in film and TV include appearances opposite Joaquin Phoenix in the film *Don't Worry, He Won't Get Far on Foot* and the role of Beth on *One Day at a Time*. She is an avid storyteller and always finds creative ways to infuse comedy into her advocacy work. *www.instagram.com/santinamuha*

JEN RAFFERTY, Founder of Empowered Educator
Jen is an educator, author and founder of Empowered Educator. Since its inception, the Empowered Educator has reached teachers and school leaders all over the world. Jen has been featured in Authority Magazine, Medium, Thrive Global, Forbes, Voyage MIA and was on the TEDx stage with her talk, Generational Change begins with Empowered Teachers. She is also the host of the podcast Take Notes with Jen Rafferty, which is rated in the top 3% of podcasts globally. *www.empowerededucator.com*
Photo: Alekandra Alekandre

CARA REEDY, Director, Disabled Journalists Association
Cara is a journalist, an actor, a director and a photographer. Previously she was the Program Manager for DREDF's Disability Media Alliance Project (DMAP). In her role as Program Manager for DMAP, Cara's mission is to have disabled people control our own narratives. The world is missing out on some of the best stories on the planet, the journalist in her knows that can't stand. She is former CNN and NPR producer and is currently developing two comedy pilots that focus on social justice. *www.infamouslyshort.com*

DALI RIVERA, Bullying Awareness & Prevention Educator
Dali is a highly skilled parenting coach with a focus on bullying awareness and prevention education for parents of middle school-age children. She equips parents with the necessary tools to effectively advocate for their children and navigate the experience in a positive and healthy way. Dali extends her services to organizations that seek to educate their communities on the importance of addressing bullying, making her an invaluable resource for promoting a safe and inclusive environment. *www.DaliTalks.com*

KIM ROXIE, CEO and Founder, LAMIK Beauty
Southern belle, seasoned makeup artist, licensed esthetician and member of the Cosmetic Executive Women (CEW), Kim is the Founder and CEO of LAMIK Beauty, a tech-enabled beauty brand that is poised to be one of the most inclusive in the market. Roxie's pivot from brick and mortar into the e-commerce and live shopping space has catapulted her to making LAMIK the first black-owned clean makeup brand carried by the major beauty specialty retailer, Ulta.com — changing the clean beauty game in Houston, Texas and beyond. *www.lamikbeauty.com*

KYLEE STONE, Brand Builder and Leadership Coach
Kylee is a Brand Builder and Leadership Coach on a mission to transform the way we listen, live and lead. A descendant of the stolen generation of the Wakka Wakka and Kulluli First Nations People, she has an intrinsic talent in connecting people with purpose to ignite their passion, grow their influence and amplify their impact. She is an award-winning leader and former Director of Marketing with over 20 years in transformational leadership and the business of storytelling, *www.ThePerformanceCode.co*

LISA THOMPSON, Mountaineering Coach, Author and Speaker
Lisa is the second American woman to summit K2, the second highest and considered the deadliest mountain in the world. She is the author of *Finding Elevation: Fear and Courage on the World's Most Dangerous Mountain* and has nearly 20 years of high-altitude mountaineering experience including multiple 8,000-meter summits and the highest mountain on all seven continents. Lisa founded Alpine Athletics, a results-based endurance coaching company that builds well-rounded mountain athletes. *www.lisaclimbs.com*

CRYSTAL LYNESE WALKER, D&I Executive
With over 15 years of experience in Corporate Diversity & Inclusion, Crystal is dedicated to creating inclusive spaces where everyone feels they belong. Outside of work, Crystal is passionate about women's liberation and empowering Black women to build thriving communities. Her interests include fashion, music, art and DIY decorating — whether it's crafting a new look or tackling a home project, she's all in. An audiobook enthusiast and tarot reading aficionado, she also has a deep love for documentaries on ancient civilizations. She believes in living life boldly, creatively and with a heart full of purpose. *www.crystallynese.com*

ERICA WRIGHT, Founder of Project U First
Erica is the founder of Project U First Inc., an organization that supports some of the most vulnerable members of our community by providing them with basic hygiene products most of us take for granted. Since its inception in 2014, UFirst has distributed more than 1 million hygiene kits, 300,000 blankets and 225,000 pairs of socks to homeless shelters, foster homes and schools in low-income areas. These items are an important step on the path toward dignity. *www.projectufirst.org*

ABOUT THE *passionistas*

HOTO BY PUPP ETZIONI

MY & NANCY HARRINGTON, Co-Founders, The Passionistas Project
'e're the Passionistas, Amy & Nancy Harrington, sisters who grew up with three older blings who were all pop culture addicts just like us. We were surrounded by creativity — t, books, music, games, cooking, theater, dancing and television.

ıt even though our dad had a successful business career, he never got over the fact that didn't pursue his dream of being a cartoonist. Had our mom been born in a different ne, she would have been the female Indiana Jones, traveling the world on archeological lventures. They chose traditional paths for the sake of the stability of our family but they ways encouraged us to take the risks that they didn't take.

ıd so we both pursued careers in the entertainment industry. Amy quickly rose up the nks to become Vice President of Post Production and Visual Effects at Warner Bros. ırking on blockbuster movies like the *Batman*, *Matrix* and *Harry Potter* franchises. ıncy founded her own graphic design firm and had a successful theater company in ıston before joining Amy in Hollywood and working on Academy Award® ad campaigns r Miramax.

e had dream jobs. We were honing our creative skills at the highest levels. We were lowing our passion for pop culture. But even though we had achieved success, the spark d gone out.

So, we decided to find a new adventure — together. But in doing so, we needed to look at what success meant to us outside of the traditional Hollywood power structure and redefine it for ourselves.

The way we had always looked at success was changing. The careers we had pursued straight out of college no longer fueled our passion. This traditional version of success wasn't fulfilling.

So we walked away from it all and found ourselves on a path of self-discovery that led us to the world of celebrity interviewing. Helping people tell their stories became our new passion. Together, we have conducted and produced over 1,600 celebrity interviews for our own website, The Interviews for the Television Academy Foundation and The Rock and Roll Hall of Fame.

In 2016, we found ourselves once again examining the meaning of success. While we loved interviewing Hollywood royalty, we couldn't ignore the changing world around us. The #MeToo and Time's Up movements were in full swing and we were in awe of the brave women stepping forward to share their very personal stories.

We knew that they needed to do something to help lift up these women, too. Now we shine a light on the positive stories of self-identified women and non-binary people through The Passionistas Project with our podcast, Power of Passionistas women's equity summit and online sisterhood.

Our goal is to inspire women to embrace their authenticity, pursue their passions and support one another along the way. We believe that by creating a space where women can connect, tell their own unfiltered stories and empower each other, they can transform their lives and change the world.

www.thepassionistasproject.com

Thank you to everyone who shared their time and wisdom with us on our journey to create this journal.

Karen Herman, your mastery with words and thoughtful insights have been a true gift. Annette Kahler, your steadfast support and unparalleled legal expertise have given us the confidence to keep moving forward. Julie DeLucca-Collins, your gentle nudge to push beyond our limits has fueled our growth. Kylee Stone, your ability to refine our message and help us define our purpose has been invaluable. Dr. Melissa Bird, you are a magical beacon who constantly reminds us to trust the messages from our souls. Lauren Best, you encourage us to listen to our intuition and treat ourselves with kindness. Crystal Lynese Walker, you remind us to always consider the experiences of others as we create an inclusive platform where everyone is free to share their authentic stories.

Thank you to all of the women we have interviewed for the Passionistas Project Podcast, especially the women quoted in these pages. Your commitment to your unique visions fuels our mission to build this worldwide community.

A huge thank you to our siblings and best friends, Beth Harrington, Lisa Barbosa and Lee Harrington, who have always inspired us to follow our passions. And a special additional thanks to Lee for his expert legal advice along the way.

And our undying gratitude to Marvin Etzioni and Rob Johnson, who always encourage us to pursue our purpose, be of service and follow our passions.

And most importantly, thank you to all of you in our Passionistas community for taking this journey with us and being part of our sisterhood.

JOIN THE PASSIONISTAS PROJECT

We are an inclusive sisterhood where passion-driven women come to get education, resources and support, find their purpose and feel empowered to transform their lives and change the world.

Sisters and Founders Amy and Nancy Harrington have created a space where trust, acceptance, inclusivity, solidarity, loyalty, honesty and authenticity are the cornerstones of their community.

The Passionistas Project online community gives women the tools they need to thrive in three key areas: business development, personal growth and social impact. Through the Passionistas Project Podcast, annual Power of Passionistas women's equity summit, books, courses, workshops, meet-ups, events and more, women and gender nonconforming nonbinary people from around the world are joining the Passionistas' mission to create a community where everyone is supported in their purpose, empowered to follow their passions and encouraged to live authentically.

Join the sisterhood.

Made in the USA
Las Vegas, NV
21 November 2024